PLANETS
AND SATELLITES

Contents

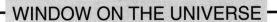

PLANETS
AND SATELLITES

Barron's Educational Series

The planets of the Solar System

The Earth is a small **planet** which revolves around the Sun, one of the 100 billion **stars** in our galaxy. Other planets, nine in all, move around the Sun, captives of its gravitational pull. Almost all the planets have **satellites** that **orbit** around them. This group, composed of the Sun, the planets and their satellites, together with a multitude of smaller bodies, principally asteroids and comets, makes up the **Solar System**.

The four planets closest to the Sun (Mercury, Venus, Earth, and Mars, in order of increasing distance) have similar characteristics and for this they are called the **terrestrial planets.** They are small, rocky bodies, with a relatively high density, and have few or no satellites. The four following planets (Jupiter, Saturn, Uranus, and Neptune) are called the **giant planets.** They are more in their original form than the terrestrial planets and consist mostly of gases.

Pluto doesn't fit in this category. It is the most distant planet, and the smallest.

Right: The Solar System was created out of interstellar material, in whose center a star, the Sun, was condensed (A). The rest of the material began to spin around it, condensing into different celestial bodies (B). The different gravitational pulls of these celestial bodies resulted in the formation of the planets and the satellites (C).

Below: From left to right in the illustration: the small, rocky planets— Mercury, Venus, Earth, Mars; the giant, gaseous planets—Jupiter, Saturn, Uranus, Neptune; and tiny Pluto.

A
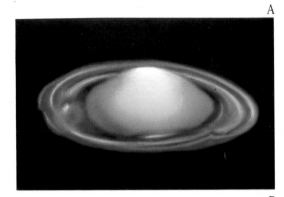

B

C
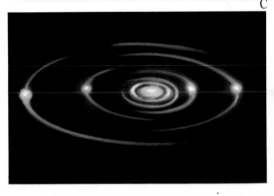

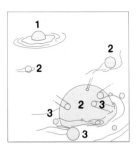

Below: The Solar System was created five billion years ago. A cloud of interstellar dust and gas began to come together due to the effects of its own gravitational pull: the first steps toward the forming of the Solar System. In its center the Sun was formed ① and afterwards the interstellar material condensed into other celestial bodies "trapped" by the gravitational pull ②. The successive condensation of material and the bombardment of **meteorites** ③ formed the early Solar System.

Mercury, the closest to the Sun

Because it is so close to the Sun, Mercury is a difficult planet to observe. It can only be observed for a maximum of two hours at dusk, after sunset, or before sunrise. A great deal of what we know about Mercury comes from the exploration carried out by the *Mariner 10* interplanetary space probe in the years 1974 and 1975 when it circled the planet three times.

Mercury's orbit around the Sun distinguishes it from the other planets by two peculiarities. For one thing, its **ecliptic** plane is more inclined than the majority of planets. Another thing is that it has a very **elliptical** orbit. When Mercury passes the **perihelion** (the point of the orbit when it is closest to the Sun), the distance to the Sun is less than two thirds of the distance when it passes by the **aphelion** (the point farthest from the Sun).

Mercury is so close to the Sun that it receives six times more solar radiation than the Earth. As you can imagine, the temperature on its illuminated side is very high.

Mercury's surface appears to be covered with craters similar to those of the Moon. The origin of these craters is the impact of meteorites of all sizes, which populated the Solar System when the planets finished forming, five billion years ago.

Mercury's craters, like those of the Moon, have remained intact all this time, thanks to the absence of *erosion*, since Mercury has no **atmosphere.**

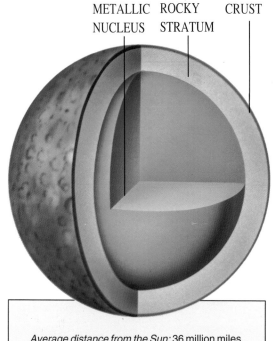

METALLIC NUCLEUS   ROCKY STRATUM   CRUST

Average distance from the Sun: 36 million miles (58 million km) (0.39 times that of Earth)
Length of year: 0.24 Earth years
Length of a day: 59 Earth days
Diameter: 3,032.4 miles (4,878 km) (0.38 times that of Earth)
Gravity: 0.37 times that of Earth
Satellites: none

Below: Mercury's surface is similar to that of the Moon, since it has numerous craters caused by the impact of meteorites. The craters have been safe from erosion because Mercury has no atmosphere. The reason for this absence of atmosphere is that the force of the planet's gravitational pull is too weak to retain atmospheric gases.

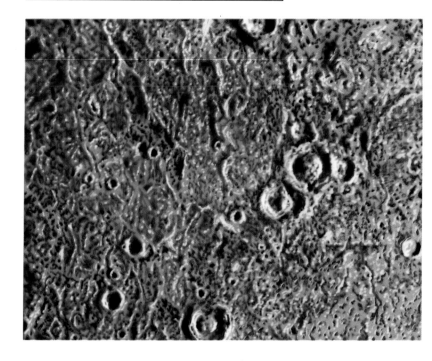

Below: Mercury is the planet closest to the Sun. Thanks to the information given to us by space probes, we know that its surface is arid and rocky and that it is furrowed with craters and mountain ranges. The light which Mercury receives from the Sun is six times more intense than the light which arrives at the Earth. During the day the temperature on Mercury exceeds 800°F (430°C).

Venus, forever covered by clouds

Venus is the planet that comes closest to the Earth, and shines very brightly in the sky. Because of its position near the Sun, it can only be seen for a few hours after sunset or before sunrise.

Venus' size and distance from the Sun makes it seem very similar to the Earth. It was believed for a long time, before its characteristics were fully known, that the planet could sustain life. However, it was discovered that it has a surface temperature of 860°F (460°C), much higher than what it logically should be when taking into account its distance from the Sun. Why is the temperature so high? The answer lies in the atmosphere of Venus.

This atmosphere is very dense. Solar light can penetrate it and heat the planet's surface, but the heat emitted from the surface cannot escape through the atmosphere. It remains trapped on the planet. This is what is known as the *greenhouse effect*, which has converted Venus into an inferno of high temperature and pressure (about 100 times that of Earth).

Venus' surface cannot be observed directly because the planet is permanently covered by a thick layer of clouds.

Venus is a planet geologically alive and probably has active volcanoes. There are mountains higher than Everest on Venus, and land formations that remind us of the continents on Earth, rising above the average level of the planet. Among them are great depressions that may at one time have been ocean beds, which evaporated long ago.

Below: The Russian interplanetary probes, called *Venera*, landed on Venus' surface and were able to transmit a few images before being destroyed after several minutes by the enormous pressure and temperature on Venus. The images transmitted by the probes show flat terrain covered with rocks, worn down by Venus' atmosphere.

CRUST   METALLIC NUCLEUS   ROCKY STRATUM

Average distance from the Sun: 67 million miles (108 million km) (0.72 times that of Earth)
Length of year: 0.62 Earth years
Length of a day: 243 Earth days
Diameter: 7,519 miles (12,104 km) (0.95 times that of Earth)
Gravity: 0.91 times that of Earth
Satellites: none

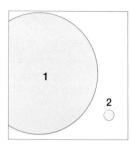

Below: Venus ① is the second planet from the Sun and the closest to the Earth ②. It is covered by a thick layer of clouds, composed of **carbon dioxide,** which prevents observation of its surface.

Earth, the blue planet

Earth is the planet which we inhabit. We're used to living on it and it's hard for us to think of it as a planet. How is it seen from space?

The first thing that stands out is its blue color. A great deal of its surface is covered by water, forming oceans. It is the only planet where water exists in liquid form.

Water is also found in the clouds in the atmosphere in the form of ice crystals, which gives them their characteristic white color. The Earth's atmosphere, composed of nitrogen and oxygen, is another of this planet's peculiarities. Compared to Venus or Mars, the Earth's atmosphere at present has little carbon dioxide. What there was initially was dissolved in the sea water and consumed by the first forms of life which appeared on the Earth. These were green sea algae, which enriched the atmosphere with oxygen.

Geologically, the Earth is a very active planet. The Earth's **crust** is divided into great plates, which are pushed by slow currents. Europe and America, which are on different plates, continue to separate a few centimeters each year.

At the bottom of the Atlantic Ocean, where the crust is thinnest, a new crust is forming. In other regions of the Earth, the plates collide, resulting in earthquakes.

The Earth is not an isolated planet. It possesses a satellite, the Moon, which stands out for its size. Its diameter is one-fourth the size of the Earth's.

Below, left: Earth's crust is formed by large plates that "float" over its **mantle.** At the bottom of the Atlantic Ocean we find the Atlantic Dorsal, a great mountain range that separates the European and American plates.

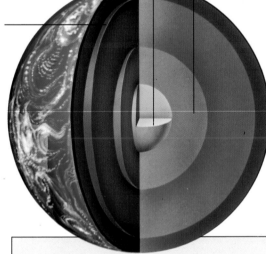

SOLID METALLIC NUCLEUS

LIQUID METALLIC NUCLEUS

CRUST

ROCKY STRATUM

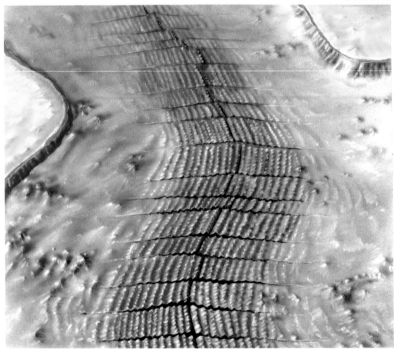

Average distance from the Sun: 93 million miles (150 million km)
Diameter: 7,926.2 miles (12,104 km)
Satellites: 1
Distance from the Earth to the Moon: 239,000 miles (384,400 km)
Diameter of the Moon: 0.27 times that of the Earth
Gravity on the Moon: 0.17 that of the Earth

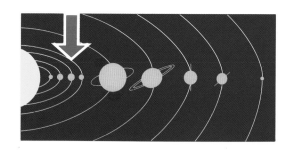

Below: The Earth seen from the surface of the Moon. From space, our planet appears as an intense blue color, due to the existence of water in liquid form. Five billion years ago, volcanic gases formed the atmosphere, and evaporated water condensed and fell in the form of rain, creating the oceans. It was in these waters where life was born.

Mars, the red planet

For a long time, it was thought that Mars, the red planet, was inhabited by extraterrestrial beings, the "martians," who had built an extensive network of "canals" on the planet's surface. It has been confirmed that there are no canals and that there has been no intelligent life on Mars.

But the interest awakened about the planet has not subsided, and, after the Moon, it will probably be the next body in the Solar System to be visited by astronauts.

Mars has been explored by interplanetary probes. The *Viking* probes, without doubt the most famous, landed on its surface in 1976.

There are indications that in the past, the planet was similar to the Earth, and had water flowing on its surface. At present, the only water there exists in the form of ice in the polar caps, or as occasional morning frost.

Mars' seasons are similar to the Earth's and the polar caps vary throughout the year. In the summer hemisphere, the extension of ice is less than in the other hemisphere. The situation is reversed after half a Martian year.

Mars has a very thin atmosphere composed mainly of carbon dioxide. Each Martian year, the changing of the seasons brings on enormous dust storms.

Below, left: Mars' two satellites, Phobos and Deimos, are very small irregular bodies. Phobos has a diameter of about 15 miles (25 km) and takes 8 hours to rotate around Mars. Deimos is even smaller.

Below: There are big mountains on the surface of Mars. Mount Olympus is the highest, at 78,000 feet (25,000 m). It is an ancient volcano, much higher than any other mountain on Earth.

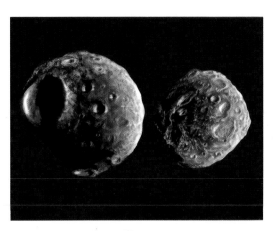

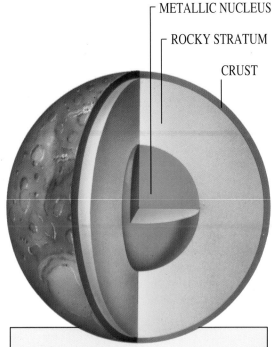

METALLIC NUCLEUS

ROCKY STRATUM

CRUST

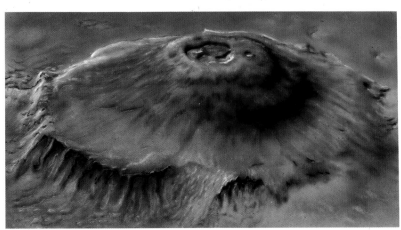

Average distance from the Sun: 142 million miles (228 million km) (1.52 times that of Earth)
Length of year: 1.88 Earth years
Length of a day: 1 Earth day
Diameter: 4,194 miles (6,787 km) (0.53 times that of Earth)
Gravity: 0.38 times that of Earth
Satellites: 2

Below: A *Viking* interplanetary probe landed on Mars' surface. The images relayed by these probes show a reddish surface covered with pebbles, dust, and rocks in various sizes. The sky's color is also red, due to the dust which floats in the air. The probes analyzed samples of the surface looking for signs of life, but the results were negative.

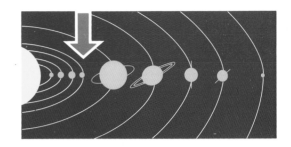

Jupiter, the giant planet

Jupiter is the giant of the Solar System. Its diameter is ten times greater than the Earth's. Its gravitational pull is so high, that it slightly affects the movement of all the other planets, and is capable of diverting many comets that come close to its orbit.

Almost all of Jupiter's interior is composed of **hydrogen** (and some **helium**) in a liquid state, compressed by the enormous weight of the atmosphere above. Near the visible surface, where the pressure is less, the hydrogen passes into a gaseous state, forming the planet's atmosphere.

The visible surface of the planet corresponds to the upper part of the clouds in the atmosphere, photographed by the interplanetary probes *Pioneer* and *Voyager* when they passed by Jupiter during their journey to the outer planets.

From the Earth, besides the structure of bands in the atmosphere, another detail of the atmosphere can be seen, the Great Red Spot situated in the southern hemisphere of the planet. The spot's reddish color is produced by the compounds of nitrogen on Jupiter.

In addition to its big family of satellites, Jupiter has a very thin ring formed by a multitude of particles, fairly close to the planet's upper cloud deck.

Below, left: Jupiter's upper atmosphere is composed of a series of light and dark bands which represent higher and lower cloud layers.

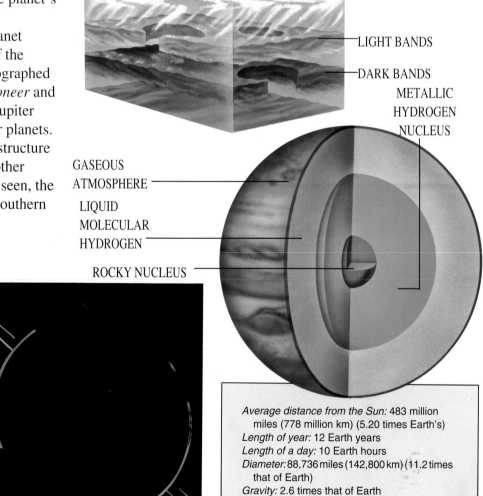

LIGHT BANDS

DARK BANDS

METALLIC HYDROGEN NUCLEUS

GASEOUS ATMOSPHERE

LIQUID MOLECULAR HYDROGEN

ROCKY NUCLEUS

Right: On the *Voyager* probe's travels to the outer planets, it captured images of Jupiter's dark side, where a thin ring surrounding the planet can be seen.

Average distance from the Sun: 483 million miles (778 million km) (5.20 times Earth's)
Length of year: 12 Earth years
Length of a day: 10 Earth hours
Diameter: 88,736 miles (142,800 km) (11.2 times that of Earth)
Gravity: 2.6 times that of Earth
Satellites: 4 big, 12 small
Rings: 1, very thin

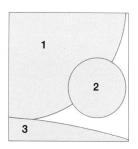

Below: Most notice-able on Jupiter's surface is the Great Red Spot, ① an immense whirlwind formed in the atmo-sphere with charac-teristics resembling those of cyclones on Earth. In the illustra-tion you can also see Jupiter's two princi-pal satellites Io ② and Europa ③.

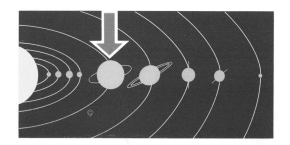

Jupiter's satellites

Jupiter has a family of numerous satellites. At present, 16 are known. Among those, the four largest stand out: Io, Europa, Ganymede, and Callisto. They are called the *Galilean satellites* because they were discovered by Galileo when he observed Jupiter with a telescope. After the Moon, the Galilean satellites are the most famous in the Solar System.

With a small telescope they can easily be observed from the Earth. They look like faint points of light lined up on one or both sides of Jupiter. The Galilean satellites were explored in detail by the *Voyager* probes, which obtained impressive images of all of them.

Io, the closest of the four to Jupiter, is an intense reddish-orange color and its surface is covered by sulphur compounds.

Europa, the satellite next closest to Jupiter, has a very smooth, bright surface, covered by ice, and furrowed by a network of dark cracks.

Ganymede is the largest satellite of the Solar System, even larger than Mercury. Its surface is quite varied, showing dark and light areas. Some craters stand out because of their whiteness, and were produced by meteorites that broke through the superficial layer of ice and dust.

Callisto is the farthest of the Galilean satellites.

Besides the four Galilean satellites, Jupiter has a multitude of small satellites. Some of them are most likely asteroids captured by Jupiter's gravitational pull.

Left: Io has numerous volcanoes, which shoot material more than 60 miles (100 km). This volcanic activity is caused by Jupiter's gravitational pull.

Left: A comparison between Earth and the Moon with the size of the Galilean satellites, from left to right, Ganymede, Callisto, Io, and Europa. The Galilean satellites, with the exception of Europa, are larger than the Moon.

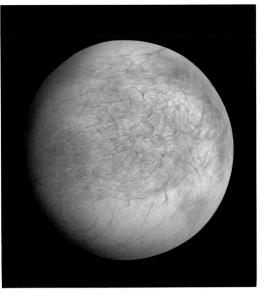

Left: Europa has an extraordinarily smooth surface, rather like an immense billiard ball. Under the surface of ice, it is believed that there could be a layer of liquid water, just like the Earth's Arctic Ocean.

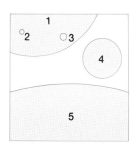

Below: Jupiter ① has 16 satellites. They can be divided into three groups: an exterior group, the four Galilean satellites, and a group of satellites inside Jupiter's ring. The four Galilean satellites are: Io ②, the satellite closest to the planet and comparable in size to the Moon, Europa ③, with its smooth covering layer of ice, Ganymede ④, the largest satellite in the Solar System; and Callisto ⑤, the moon whose surface contains the most craters.

Saturn, a spectacular planet

Saturn's magnificent rings make this planet unmistakable. Even with a small telescope it is possible to see the little disk of Saturn surrounded by its rings. Saturn seems so small when seen from the Earth because it is almost twice as far away as Jupiter. In reality, the two planets are similar in size, although Saturn is slightly smaller.

What makes Saturn stand out is its low density: it is the only planet in the Solar System less dense than water. If we were to put Saturn in a bathtub full of water, it would float! The problem is finding a bathtub big enough.

Saturn is the planet with the most satellites. It has a total of 23, many of them extraordinarily small, discovered by *Voyager* probes when they passed close to Saturn. The biggest and most interesting of these satellites is Titan.

Titan has a considerable atmosphere formed for the most part of nitrogen and methane, which prevent its surface from being seen. It is believed that the methane on Titan may play a similar role to that of water on the Earth. It could be present in solid or liquid form on the surface and in the form of a gas in the atmosphere. Titan is one of the bodies in the Solar System that will be explored in the future to see if some form of life inhabits the satellite using methane as the basis of life instead of water.

The other four large satellites (Rhea, Iapetus, Dione, and Tethys) have diameters of about 650 miles (1,000 km) with an appearance similar to the Galilean satellites of Jupiter.

Left, below: The surface of Mimas is partially covered by the crater Herschel, which was formed as a result of a tremendous impact which almost shattered the satellite into pieces.

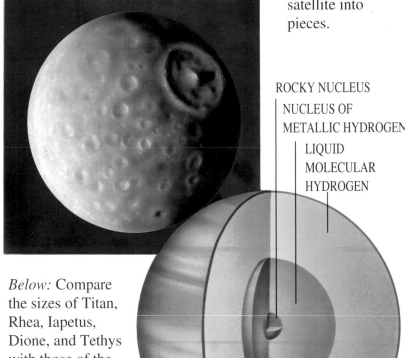

ROCKY NUCLEUS

NUCLEUS OF METALLIC HYDROGEN

LIQUID MOLECULAR HYDROGEN

Below: Compare the sizes of Titan, Rhea, Iapetus, Dione, and Tethys with those of the Earth and the Moon.

Average distance from the Sun: 887.14 million miles (1,424 million km) (9.52 times Earth's)
Length of year: 29 Earth years
Length of a day: 10 Earth hours
Diameter: 74,978 miles (120,000 km) (9.4 times that of Earth)
Gravity: 1.1 times that of Earth
Satellites: 5 big ones, 18 small
Rings: 3 major divisions

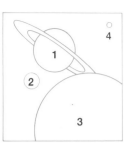

Below: Saturn ①, with its system of rings, is the most spectacular planet of the Solar System. It also has the greatest number of satellites (23). In the illustration you can see Tethys ②, and Dione ③, two of the most important, and Mimas ④ which stands out because of its crater.

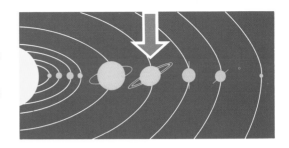

Saturn's rings

All of the giant planets, Jupiter, Saturn, Uranus, and Neptune, have rings. But none of them compares with the rings of Saturn. Without doubt, these are the most spectacular and most impressive show in the Solar System.

Saturn's rings extend from close to the surface to more than twice the radius of the planet [about 87,000 miles (140,000 kilometers)].

You can see them easily from Earth with a small telescope, although every 15 years they stop being visible. It is then while in its orbit around the Sun, Saturn's position is such that its rings present themselves edge-on. The rings are so thin that when this happens, they cannot be seen from the Earth.

For a long time it was known that Saturn's rings were not solid. They are formed by a large quantity of small particles (from the size of dust particles to the size of a small house) mostly composed of ice. They move around Saturn following circular paths lined up with the planet's equator. Some of the material remains dispersed, unable to form satellites due to its proximity to the planet.

From the Earth, three principal rings can be distinguished. The most exterior is *ring A*, which is separated from *ring B* by the Cassini Division, an empty space between both rings. Ring A has its own division, called Encke, which is much narrower than that of Cassini. Closer to Saturn's surface we see *ring C*, thinner than the others.

The rings have turned out to be much more complex than was believed before they were explored by the *Voyager* probe. More rings have been discovered,

in particular the *ring F*, formed by two or three braided threads. Each ring, it turns out, is composed of thousands of very narrow rings, and not all the divisions are completely empty space. *Voyager's* images of Saturn's rings are reminiscent of an immense phonograph record.

Below, left: The ring F owes its unusual braided form to the presence of small satellites, called *shepherd satellites*, next to the ring.

Below: The most brilliant ring is B, which is separated from the A ring by the Cassini Division. Other fainter rings, C and D, are closer to Saturn.

Below: Saturn's ring system is one of the most spectacular phenomena of the Solar System. The thickness of the different fringes or rings is only a few miles. Each ring is formed by a great number of ice particles, each probably with a rocky **nucleus.** The size of these particles ranges from a little more than a fraction of an inch to close to 30 feet. These celestial bodies rotate around the planet, following circular orbits above Saturn's equator. The planet's gravitational pull prevents the particles from grouping and forming a satellite too close to Saturn.

Uranus, the first discovered with a telescope

Situated at a distance from the Sun almost twice that of Saturn, we find Uranus. It is one of the giant planets, although not as big as Jupiter or Saturn.

Uranus was unknown in ancient times, and was the first planet to be discovered with a telescope. In fact, it can be seen with the naked eye, but without a big telescope, you wouldn't be able to distinguish the planet's disk.

One of Uranus' notable characteristics is that the planet's rotation axis lies on the plane of its orbit around the Sun. In this way, Uranus' poles successively line up towards the Sun every half a Uranian year (every 42 Earth years). The rest of the planets have their axes more or less perpendicular to the ecliptic plane.

Uranus is also, next to Saturn, the first planet where rings were discovered. In 1977 five thin rings around Uranus were observed from the Earth, while Uranus was passing in front of a distant but very brilliant star, which briefly covered its light.

Five satellites belonging to Uranus have been observed from the Earth, but little can be learned about them from such a great distance. *Voyager* observed them in detail and also discovered 10 new satellites.

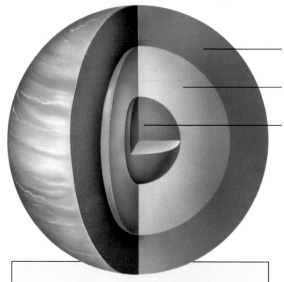

GASEOUS ATMOSPHERE

HELIUM MANTLE

ROCKY NUCLEUS

Average distance from the Sun: 1,784 million miles (2,870 million km) (19.2 times Earth's)
Length of one year: 84 Earth years
Length of a day: 17 Earth hours
Diameter: 32,200 miles (51,2000 km) (4 times that of the Earth)
Gravity: 0.9 times that of the Earth
Satellites: 4 big ones, 11 small ones
Rings: 11, very narrow and dark

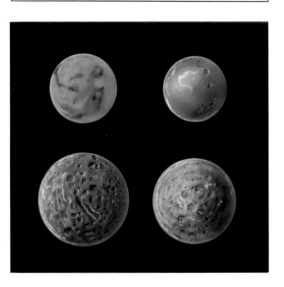

Below, left: Uranus' rings, discovered from the Earth, are very thin and dark. The *Voyager* interplanetary probe observed a total of 11 rings around Uranus when it passed by the planet.

Left: Uranus' four major satellites each have diameters of slightly less than 1,000 miles. They are similar to Jupiter's Galilean satellites. From left to right and from above to below, are Ariel, Umbriel, Titania, and Oberon.

Below: Uranus ①, seen from the surface of Miranda ②. Uranus' blue color is due to the methane in its atmosphere. Miranda, a medium sized satellite belonging to Uranus, has a surface of high mountains and deep chasms.

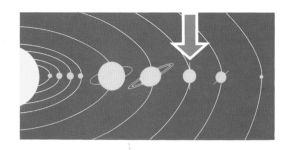

Neptune, the farthest giant planet

Neptune was the first planet to be discovered as a result of its effect on the orbit of another planet, in this case, Uranus.

Neptune was the planet most recently visited by the *Voyager* interplanetary probe at the end of its twelve year journey through the Solar System. Neptune is so far away from us (30 times the distance from the Earth to the Sun) that it was poorly observed from the Earth.

Voyager's images have revealed a planet with an intense blue color, caused by the methane contained in its atmosphere, which is composed primarily of hydrogen and helium. Unlike Uranus, Neptune's atmosphere demonstrates great activity, with a structure of bands, a large dark spot similar to Jupiter's, and small white clouds.

Neptune, like all the giant planets, has rings. From the Earth only incomplete pieces of the rings were seen, but *Voyager* revealed that the rings are complete with some parts brighter than others.

From the Earth, the existence of two satellites, Nereid and Triton, was known. The *Voyager* probe discovered six more, all very small.

Below: Triton and Nereid are Neptune's largest satellites. Triton is almost as big as the Moon and Nereid has a diameter of about 200 miles (300 km).

GASEOUS ATMOSPHERE ROCKY NUCLEUS HELIUM MANTLE

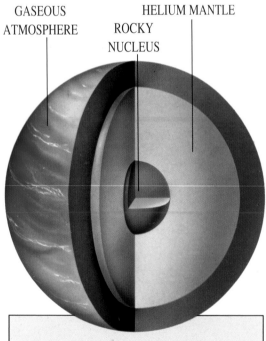

Below: Triton's surface has many narrow valleys, craters and peaks, and frozen lakes of volcanic origin.

Average distance from the Sun: 2,796 million miles (4,492 million km). (30 times Earth's)
Length of a year: 165 Earth years
Length of a day: 16 Earth hours
Diameter: 30,775 miles (48,700 km) (3.8 times that of the Earth)
Gravity: 1.2 times that of the Earth
Satellites: 2 big ones, 6 small ones
Rings: 4, narrow

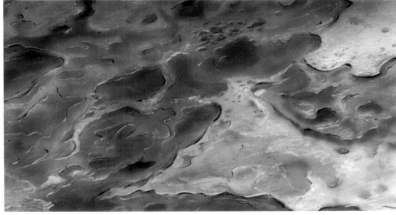

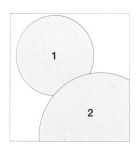

Below: Neptune ① and its biggest satellite, Triton ②. This satellite rotates in the reverse direction around Neptune, a unique case among the big satellites of the Solar System. It is possible that Triton was formed as an independent body and then was captured by Neptune.

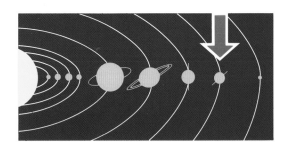

Pluto and beyond

Pluto, the ninth planet of the Solar System, is the only one which hasn't been visited by an interplanetary probe, and it probably won't be explored for many years. For this reason, we know less about Pluto than any other planet.

Pluto was discovered fairly recently, in 1930, due to some irregularities in Neptune's orbit. These irregularities were attributed to the presense of an unknown planet that turned out to be Pluto.

It orbit is very inclined and very eccentric compared to the other planets. Therefore, although Pluto is on the average the planet farthest from the Sun, during 20 of the 248 years that it takes to travel around the Sun it is closer to the Sun than is Neptune.

Pluto doesn't resemble any of the four giant planets, and is much farther from the Sun than the four terrestrial planets. Pluto is the smallest of the planets (its diameter is half that of Mercury's) and its composition is similar to Triton's, the largest of Neptune's satellites.

Since Pluto's discovery, the question of whether or not the Solar System might have another planet beyond Pluto has been raised. Presently, it is believed that there is no other, unless it is very small. If it exists, it would be discovered by any influence it might have upon the trajectories of the interplanetary probes *Pioneer* and *Voyager*, which have traveled much farther than Pluto's orbit.

METHANE SURFACE   ROCKY NUCLEUS   FROZEN METHANE

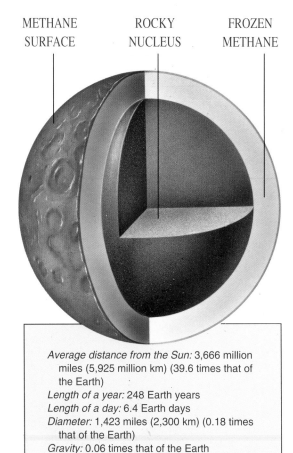

Left: Pluto has a composition similar to Triton, one of Neptune's satellites. It is covered by a thin layer of frozen methane. Pluto's very thin atmosphere is composed of methane.

Average distance from the Sun: 3,666 million miles (5,925 million km) (39.6 times that of the Earth)
Length of a year: 248 Earth years
Length of a day: 6.4 Earth days
Diameter: 1,423 miles (2,300 km) (0.18 times that of the Earth)
Gravity: 0.06 times that of the Earth
Satellites: 1

Left: Charon, Pluto's only satellite, was discovered in 1978. Its size is very large in relation to Pluto. The rest of the satellites are much smaller than the planets they orbit, with the exception of the Moon, which is one-fourth the size of the Earth.

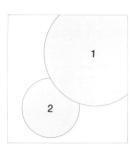

Below: Pluto ① is the planet farthest from the Sun and the smallest. It has a satellite called Charon ②, which is an exceptionally large satellite when compared to the size of Pluto. It is more than half of Pluto's size.

Activity: a model of the Solar System

What does the Solar System look like from the outside? How are the planets separated from each other? The best way to answer these questions would be to construct a model of the Solar System and place objects where the Sun and the planets would be. You should use the same scale for the sizes of the objects, the distances between the planets, and their distances from the Sun.

You can use a big ball, for example a basketball (approximately 25 centimeters or 10 inches in diameter) to represent the Sun. On this scale the terrestrial planets would have to be represented with heads of pins and marbles.

Although you only want to construct a model of the Solar System's interior corresponding to the terrestrial planets, the distance at which you would have to put Mars—as you can see in the box below—would be very great.

If you wanted to represent the whole Solar System using this scale, Jupiter would have a diameter of 2.5 centimeters (a big marble) and would be placed 143 meters from the Sun, Neptune 823 meters, and Pluto a distance of more than 1,083 meters.

DIAMETERS AND DISTANCES FROM THE SUN (Approximate scale 1:560 million) 2.5 cm ≈ 1 in. 1m ≈ 3.3 ft			
	Diameter	Object	Distance from the Sun
Sun	25 cm	Basketball	—
Mercury	1 mm	Small pinhead	11 m
Venus	2 mm	Big pinhead	20 m
Earth	2 mm	Big pinhead	27 m
Mars	1 mm	Small pinhead	42 m
Jupiter	2.5 cm	Big marble	143 m
Saturn	2 cm	Medium marble	256 m
Uranus	1 cm	Small marble	526 m
Neptune	1 cm	Small marble	823 m
Pluto	0.5 mm	Small pinhead	1,083 m

Below: Compare the sizes of the planets in relation to the Sun, which is hardly visible in the illustration. They are, in order of their proximity to the Sun: Mercury ①, Venus ②, Earth ③, Mars ④, Jupiter ⑤, Saturn ⑥, Uranus ⑦, Neptune ⑧, Pluto ⑨.

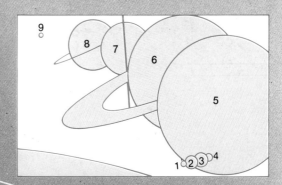

Glossary

aphelion: The point on a planet's orbit farthest from the Sun.

atmosphere: A layer of gases surrounding most planets and some satellites.

carbon dioxide: Gas composed of carbon and oxygen. This gas is the most abundant one in the atmosphere of Venus and Mars.

crust: The layer of the planet found closest to its surface.

ecliptic: The plane on which the orbits of almost all the planets in the Solar System can be found.

ellipse: The form of the orbits made by the planets as they circle around the Sun.

giant planets: The name given to the four largest planets that are composed almost entirely of gasses: Jupiter, Saturn, Uranus, and Neptune.

helium: Gaseous element found in abundance in the Sun and giant planets.

hydrogen: The simplest of all elements, its atoms are formed of one proton and one electron. It is the most abundant element in the universe, particularly in the Sun and the giant planets.

mantle: Part of the interior of a planet, located beneath the outer shell.

meteorite: Small fragments of interplanetary matter that fall on a planet. If a meteorite is large, it will produce a crater in the area where it lands.

nucleus: Deepest interior part of a planet.

orbit: Trajectory followed by a planet as it circles the Sun, or a satellite as it circles a planet.

perihelion: The point on a planet's orbit closest to the Sun.

planet: One of the nine bodies spinning around the Sun. These differ from stars in that they don't produce their own light. They are illuminated by the Sun.

satellite: Body that revolves around a planet. All the planets except Mercury and Venus have satellites. The Moon is the Earth's satellite.

Solar System: Group consisting of the Sun, the nine planets and their satellites, and lesser bodies such as asteroids and comets.

star: Celestial body that emits its own light. The Sun is a star.

terrestrial planets: The name given to the four planets closest to the Sun. They are small in size and have a rocky composition similar to Earth: Mercury, Venus, Earth, and Mars.

Index

English translation © Copyright 1993 by Barron's
Educational Series, Inc.
The title of the Spanish Edition is *Planetas y Satélites*

© Copyright 1992 by PARRAMON EDICIONES, S.A.
First edition, April 1993
Published by Parramón Ediciones, S.A.,
Barcelona, Spain.

Author: Robert Estalella
Illustrator: Marcel Socías

All inquiries should be addressed to:
Barron's Educational Series, Inc.
250 Wireless Boulevard
Hauppauge, New York 11788

Library of Congress Catalog Card No. 93-18068

International Standard Book No. 0-8120-1737-4 (P)
0-8120-6372-4 (H)

Library of Congress Cataloging-in-Publication Data
Available on request.

Printed in Spain
3456   987654321